THE ADVENT
WREATH

AN ADVENT TRADITION OF HOPE, FAITH, HOSPITALITY AND PROMISE

CATHERINE FOURNIER

Book design and graphics by Catherine Fournier

Prayers for the Weeks of Advent adapted from the The Hours of the Divine Office.

The contents and images contained in this booklet are for your personal family use only. Help protect intellectual property and support Catholic writers by not copying.

Text and Images:
Copyright 2015 Domestic Church Communications Ltd.

WHAT IS THE ADVENT WREATH?

We've all seen them. Large circles of greenery with purple and pink candles in the Church's sanctuary, smaller versions of family dinner tables, icons and images on web-sites; they seem to be everywhere during the Advent season.

When I converted from the Presbyterian tradition which - in my childhood anyway, didn't have the Advent wreath - to Catholicism, our parish didn't have an Advent wreath. So when Advent wreaths started to show up in Catholic churches, I thought the Advent wreath was a new tradition, a post-Vatican II invention to involve the laity in the liturgy. I was both open and sceptical about this "new" tradition.

But I was wrong.

INTRODUCTION

The Advent wreath is a very old tradition. Its current form dates back at least 400 years and its actual origins are so old that they can't be dated at all.

In fact, it was pre-Christian Germanic peoples who, as the cold and dark of Winter advanced, placed lit candles within circles of greenery as a sign and invocation of the warmth, light, and life of Spring.

Further north in Scandinavia, still in pre-Christian times, lighted candles were placed around a wheel, and prayers were offered to the god of light to turn "the wheel of the earth" back toward the sun to lengthen the days and restore warmth.

By the Middle Ages, after Christianity had moved into and converted these pagan territories, Christians adapted this ancient tradition and used Advent wreaths as part of their spiritual preparation for Christmas. After all, Christ is "the Light that came into the world" to dispel the darkness of sin and to radiate the truth and love of God (cf. John 3:19-21).

And by 1600, both Catholics and Lutherans had more formal practices surrounding the Advent wreath.

HOW DO WE "DO" THE ADVENT WREATH?

The Catechism of the Catholic Church says:
*#524 When the Church celebrates the liturgy of Advent
each year, she makes present this ancient expectancy of the
Messiah, for by sharing in the long preparation for the Saviour's
first coming, the faithful renew their ardent desire for his
second coming.*

So we can see from this that Advent is:

- a preparatory season,
- a penitential season, and
- a season of anticipation.

The Advent wreath is just one of many family activities that
help create the Advent sense of preparation, penance and
anticipation.

- Its circular shape symbolizes eternity because it has no
  beginning and no end. It reminds us that God's love is
  eternal.

- Its evergreens are symbolic of life. Combined with the
  representation of eternity, it reminds us of our promise of
  eternal life in heaven.

- Its candles symbolize the light of Christ coming into the
  world. There are four candles in an Advent wreath, one for
  each week of Advent.

- The three purple or violet candles represent prayer,
  penance, and the good works of Advent as well as the
  royalty of Christ, as the Son of the Lord.

- The rose or pink candle, lit on the Third week of Advent,
  represents the hope and coming joy of the second half of
  the Advent season.

- The progressive lighting of the candles symbolizes the hope
  surrounding our Lord's first coming into the world and the
  anticipation of His second coming to judge the living and
  the dead.

In a parish setting, the Advent wreath is lit either on the first
Sunday Mass of each week and left to burn for all following

Masses, or light as part of the opening prayers of each Mass.

Family Advent wreaths are typically lit daily. At a certain time each day (either before saying Grace at dinner, or before beginning evening prayers) the candle or candles are lit. All other lights are put out and the gentle glow and flicker of the candles lights the room. The family says prayers for the grace of a good and holy preparation for Christmas may be said, sing an Advent hymn or song in honor of Mary.

In our family, the Advent wreath is placed at the centre of the family dinner table beginning on the First Sunday of Advent and for every evening of Advent. Peter blesses it and us on the First Sunday of Advent and we take turns lighting the candles every evening before we say Grace. We eat by the light of the Advent wreath alone.

In some European countries, it is traditional for family members with the name of John or Joan to first light the Advent candles, because the Gospel of John begins by calling Christ the "Light of the World" and John the Baptist was the first to recognize the light of divinity shining around the Lord at His baptism in the Jordan.

Among other things, the family Advent wreath captures the imagination and enhances the growing faith of our children.

It "incarnates" or "brings to life" the faith and teachings of the Church for them, and makes the season of Advent more real.

It is easy, during those dark dinner-times, to talk about the first long Advent when we "walked in darkness" and as the light of the candles gradually increases, to talk about the revelation and revolution of the coming of Christ for God's people.

The flicker of the candles gently draws the family's attention away from the glitter of Christmas materialism and towards the eternal light of Heaven.

HOW TO USE THIS BOOK

However you like!

In this book, I have described how to add the Advent Wreath to your family evening gathering - at dinner or evening prayers - and presented four ways to create a family Advent Wreath, beginning with a very simple put-four-candles-on-a-plate and finishing with a very elegant, but complicated hanging wreath.

All the instructional photos were taken in my kitchen, using the materials that I had around the house and in my Christmas boxes. I hope the imperfect nature of both the wreaths and the images encourage you to try these crafts yourself.

I don't know about you, but I have a terrible time trying to come up with prayers on the spur of the moment (especially when facing a table ringed with expectant or sceptical children!), so I have also included:

1. Prayers for blessing your Advent wreath,

2. Family prayers for the Sundays of Advent,

3. Daily prayers for each of the four weeks of Advent, and

4. Four weekly meditations about Advent:

   a. The first candle, alone in the darkness, evokes mankind's long wait for the Messiah.
   b. Two lit candles leads us to consider that Christ said, "Where there are two or more of you gathered in my Name, there also shall I be."
   c. Three candles begin to triumph over darkness, and reminds us of the three members of both the Trinity and the Holy Family.
   d. Four candles are bright enough to drive back the darkness, encouraging us to evangelize and share the good news with our neighbors!

Have a blessed Advent!

SOME ADVENT HYMNS AND SONGS IN MARY'S HONOUR

O COME, DIVINE MESSIAH

O come, divine Messiah,
The world in silence waits the day,
When hope shall sing its triumph,
And sadness flee away.

Refrain:
Sweet Savior, haste;
Come, come to earth:
Dispel the night and show thy face,
And bid us hail the dawn of grace.

Refrain

O thou, whom nations sighed for,
Whom priests and prophets long foretold,
Wilt break the captive fetters,
Redeem the long lost fold.

Refrain

Shalt come in peace and meekness,
And lowly will thy cradle be:
All clothed in human weakness,
Shall we thy Godhead see.

The Advent Wreath

THE ANGEL GABRIEL FROM HEAVEN CAME

The angel Gabriel from Heaven came,
His wings as drifted snow, his eyes as flame:
"From God, all hail", the angel said to Mary,
"Mostly highly favored lady."

Glo-r-ia!

"Fear not, for you shall bear a holy child,
By whom we shall to God be reconciled:
His name shall be Emmanuel, the long foretold:
Mostly highly favored lady."

Glo-r-ia!

Then gentle Mary humbly bowed her head:
"To me be as it pleases God", she said,
"My soul shall praise and magnify his holy Name."
"Mostly highly favored lady."

Glo-r-ia!

Of her Emmanuel, the Christ, was born
In Bethlehem, upon that Christmas morn,
And Christian folk throughout the world will ever
say:
"Mostly highly favored lady."

Glo-r-ia!

The Advent Wreath

O COME, O COME, EMMANUEL

O come, O come, Emmanuel,
And ransom captive Israel,
That mourns in lonely exile here,
Until the Son of God appear.

Refrain:
Rejoice! Rejoice! Emmanuel,
Shall come to thee, O Israel.

O come, thou Rod of Jesse, free,
Thine own from Satan's tyranny.
From depths of hell Thy people save,
And give them vict'ry o'er the grave.

Refrain

O come, O Dayspring, come and cheer,
Our spirits by Thine advent here.
And drive away the shades of night,
And pierce the clouds and bring us light.

Refrain

O come, Thou Key of David, come,
And open wide our Heavenly home.
Make safe the way that leads on high,
And close the path to misery.

Refrain

O come, O come, Thou Lord of might,
Who to Thy tribes, on Sinai's height,
In ancient times did'st give the law,
In cloud and majesty and awe.

IMMACULATE MARY

THE LOURDES HYMN

It is not clear who wrote the words for Immaculate Mary, known as the "Lourdes Hymn" (though I suspect it was spontaneously created during one of the apparitions of our Lady of Lourdes by a faithful spectator!) The music is a traditional French tune, with the refrain added.

Immaculate Mary, your praises we sing, who reignest in splendor with Jesus our King.

Refrain:
Ave, Ave, Ave Maria, Ave, Ave Maria.

In heaven, the blessed your glory proclaim;
On earth, we your children invoke your fair name.

Refrain

Your name is our power, your virtues our light,
Your love is our comfort, Your pleading our might.

Refrain

We pray for our mother, the Church upon earth; And bless, dearest Lady, the land of our birth.

SALVE REGINA

Hail! holy Queen enthroned above, O Maria!
Hail! Mother of Mercy and of love, O Maria!

Refrain:
Triumph, all ye cherubim,
Sing with us, ye seraphim.
Heav'n and earth resound the hymn. Salve, salve,
salve Regina!

Our life, our sweetness here below, O Maria!
Our hope in sorrow and in woe, O Maria!

Refrain

To thee we cry, poor sons of Eve, O Maria! To
thee we sigh, we mourn, we grieve, O Maria!

Refrain

This earth is but a vale of tears, O Maria! A
place of banishment, of fears, O Maria!

Refrain

Turn then, most gracious advocate, O Maria!
Toward us thine eyes compassionate, O Maria!

Refrain

When this our exile is complete, O Maria!
Show us thy, Son, our Jesus sweet, O Maria!

Refrain

O clement, gracious, Mother sweet, O Maria! O
Virgin Mary, we entreat, O Maria!

11/30/2025

THE FIRST WEEK OF ADVENT: HISTORY AND TRADITION

During the first week of Advent, only one purple candle is lit.

This is a very powerful teaching moment, especially for children. Children are fascinated with candles and candlelight. Our children "got" the message right away. It wasn't our idea to eat by its light alone, it was theirs. They insisted that we turn off all the other lights.

The single candle seems very feeble and lonely, as if its light will never overcome the surrounding darkness. It reminds us that the world waited for a very long time for the light of Christ, and of the faithful all over the world who are living in isolation or hostility.

Though we often forget, Advent is a penitential season. It's sometimes called the "little Lent."

The Advent Wreath

While there is not the same obligation to fasting, prayer and almsgiving as there is in Lent, Advent is still a time to be penitent, not celebratory. "Angel Trees" at the mall, food drives at school, and special Christmas dinners for the homeless are a few remnants in our society of the penitential nature of Advent.

In our family while we may not fast as much as during Lent, we do save our Christmas feasting for the proper time – the Christmas season. So, while I start the Christmas cooking and baking after St. Nicholas Day, we try, as much as possible, hold off serving Christmas goodies until the Christmas season between Christmas Day and Epiphany.

This is a true Advent sacrifice for our children. They find it very difficult to come home from school to the smell of Christmas cookies and not be able to eat them!

We're not not being "Scrooges", though. We've found that having and observing an awareness of the penitential aspect of Advent makes the celebration of Christmas all the more joyful and memorable.

BLESSING THE ADVENT WREATH

On the first Sunday of Advent, sprinkle the wreath with holy water and bless it before the first purple candle is lit. Say a prayer as the candles are lit every day, followed by the blessing before meals, if you use the wreath at mealtime.

Here are some suggestions for prayers.

BLESSING FOR THE ADVENT WREATH

O God, by whose word all things are made holy, pour forth your graces and blessings on this wreath. Grant that we who use it prepare our hearts for the coming of Christ, and receive abundant graces from You.

Through Christ Our Lord.
Amen.

PRAYER FOR THE FIRST SUNDAY OF ADVENT

Rouse up Your power, Lord, and come. Protect us, and we shall be rescued from the perils to which our sins are exposing us; deliver us and we shall be saved.

This we ask of You, Lord Jesus living.
Amen.

PRAYER FOR THE FIRST WEEK OF ADVENT

May the only-begotten Son of God bless us and help us as we wait for His coming.
Amen.

A SIMPLE ADVENT WREATH

This is the simplest type of Advent Wreath.

MATERIALS

- ⸙ A large plate, platter or cake stand
- ⸙ Four candlesticks
- ⸙ Three purple candles
- ⸙ One pink candle
- ⸙ Four white candles (optional)
- ⸙ Artificial garland, holly branches, branches from an artificial tree, pine cones, artificial berries, christmas tree decorations, ribbons, other decorative items.

DIRECTIONS

1. To make the wreath, arrange the candlesticks on the tray. The tray allows the wreath to be moved easily.

The Advent Wreath

2. Place the candles in the candlesticks, then place the greenery around the candles in a pleasant arrangement.

3. If you want, embellish your wreath with red berries, a small creche, ribbons or whatever else you have available.

THE SECOND WEEK OF ADVENT: COMMUNITY AND COMMUNION

During the second week of Advent, beginning with the second Sunday of Advent, we light two candles at dinner time. We remember that Christ said, "Where there are two or more of you gathered in my Name, there also shall I be."

"Two or more gathered in my name" is a classic expression of the "body of Christ" and "communion of saints". Many wonderful saints' days are scattered throughout the Advent season; St. Nicholas, St. Lucy, Immaculate Conception, and Our Lady of Guadeloupe to name a few. They're all worth observing, especially the feast of St. Nicholas.

Santa Claus, Saint Nicholas' alter ego, that jolly elf, may well be the family's biggest hindrance to a faithful Christmas. His focus is on gifts, greed, spending, not on the Nativity. He's the secular symbol of Christmas and has no place in our homes.

But Santa Claus has such a powerful presence in modern culture's Christmas celebration. He's the figure around whom all the mystery, suspense and anticipation of Christmas is focused. Aren't we taking all the joy and fun out of Christmas by "getting rid of Santa"?

Not at all. In fact, we've found that celebrating the feast of Saint Nicholas has made our Advent and Christmas more joyful. It's one of the most important - and fun! - things we do to reclaim a Catholic Advent and Christmas.

Besides, we're not "getting rid of something", we're replacing something of dubious value with a truly Catholic celebration. When we replace Santa with Saint Nicholas, the Bishop of Myra, patron of children and famous for giving gifts, and replace the stocking gifts one Christmas Eve to stocking gifts on the morning of December 6th:

- ⚜ We replace a myth with reality,

- ⚜ We break the link between Christmas and presents and now have a chance to move the focus of Christmas from gifts to the Gift of the Incarnation,

- ⚜ We reduce the size, number and grandeur of the gifts at both Saint Nicholas Day and Christmas, because the two gift categories – Santa gifts and family gifts – are no longer competing with each other. Everyone's expectations of gifts is lowered to a more reasonable level.

- ⚜ Our children get gifts three weeks before their friends at school!

For our family, this is the day that Advent really begins in earnest. I especially like that we start with a little "party gathering" at a time of day when we don't normally spend time together.

And, of course, our wreath has center place in our St. Nicholas morning feast.

PRAYER FOR THE SECOND SUNDAY OF ADVENT

Lord, make our hearts more diligent in preparing the way for Your Only-begotten Son.

His coming will help us serve You with purified souls.

This we ask of You through HIm, who lives.

Amen.

PRAYER FOR THE SECOND WEEK OF ADVENT

May Christ bring us the joys of everlasting life.

Amen.

A FRESH WREATH

This is a very nice wreath, only a little more complicated than the Simple Advent Wreath. The fresh greenery brings its pleasant aroma to the dinner table.

A fresh wreath requires:

MATERIALS

- ᛞ Shallow bowl or dish
- ᛞ Oasis (also known as florist's foam, it's available from any florist)
- ᛞ Three purple candles
- ᛞ One pink candle
- ᛞ Four white candles (optional)
- ᛞ Fresh pine boughs, cedar boughs, holly with berries or ivy
- ᛞ Small knife for carving holes in the oasis
- ᛞ Ribbon, pine cones, small ornaments

DIRECTIONS

1. Soak the oasis in warm water until it is completely saturated.

2. Fit it into the bowl, carving it and packing it in tightly as necessary so that it will not shift around.

3. Carve four holes in the oasis for the candles. Don't worry, the holes don't need to be neat!

4. Place the candles in the holes you have made and begin sticking greenery into the oasis to completely cover it.

5. Arrange the greenery so that some is trailing over the edges of the bowl, and pack it closely around the candles to hide all the foam.

6. When you've finished adding the greenery, embellish your wreath with ribbons, pine cones, and small ornaments. None, some or lots! just as seems good to you.

7. Keep the foam well watered, and try not to let the candles burn down so low that they scorch the greenery. The wreath will last from the first Sunday of Advent until Epiphany.

THE STORY OF ST. NICHOLAS

Saint Nicholas was the bishop of a city named Myra in Turkey in the early part of the fourth century. His feast day is December 6th because he died on December 6 or 7 in the middle of the fourth century. Feast days celebrate the entry of the saint's soul into Heaven.

The most famous story told about St. Nicholas has to do with three young sisters who were very poor. Their parents were so poor that they did not have enough money for the daughters to get married. Every young girl needed money to pay for the wedding and to set up house for themselves.

Nicholas heard about this family and wanted to help them, but he did not want anyone to know that he was the one who was helping them.

The story is told in a few different ways.

In one version, he climbed up on their roof three nights in a row and threw gold coins down their chimney so that they would land in the girls' stockings, which had been hung by the fire to dry. After two of his daughters had been able to marry because of the money mysteriously appearing in their stockings, the father was determined to find out who was helping them, so he hid behind the chimney the next night. Along came Bishop Nicholas with another bag of money.

When he was discovered, he asked the father not to tell anyone else, but the father wanted everyone to know what a good and generous man the Bishop Nicholas was, so he told everyone he knew.

That is how we have the story and the tradition of stocking full of gifts today.

THE THIRD WEEK OF ADVENT: HOSPITALITY

It's Gaudete Sunday – when the Gospel readings move from sorrowful preparation to joyful anticipation. On our Advent wreath the third candle – the pink one -- is lit. Now, more than half of the candles are lit! It's a visible demonstration that Light has, indeed, triumphed over darkness!

The three candles also remind us of the three members of the Holy Family. Representations of the Holy Family – in crèches – are a familiar Christmas decoration, even for those who aren't particularly devout.

The oldest known nativity scene is a wall decoration in the Roman catacombs of Saint Sebastian that was probably painted around 380, though our version of the Christmas creche was "invented" by Saint Francis of Assisi in 1293 as a way to help people "reclaim" the true meaning of Christmas.

Have we heard that one before?

Saint Francis of Assisi famously said, "Preach the Gospel unceasingly. When necessary, use words."

Saint Francis believed that a visual representation and re-enactment of Christmas night – in other words, incarnating it, making it physically real – would inspire faith and devotion in the people who saw it. He was right. Soon every church and village had its own "presepio." Saint Francis' original, by the way, featured live animals and actors, including an infant on Christmas morning.

Just one of the many lessons a presepio can teach us is a lesson in hospitality.

Luke's Nativity narrative tells us that Mary and Joseph had guests within hours of Jesus' birth. But they had nothing to offer their guests, no food, no drink, not even a comfortable place to sit down. Nothing. They weren't, they couldn't be, the perfect hosts.

And who were their guests? Several smelly shepherds. Not what you'd think of as perfect guests.

Yet, we're sure, Mary and Joseph welcomed them in. They opened their "door" and more importantly, they opened their "heart" to these most humble members of their society. They actually were – in the truest sense – perfect hosts.

Their example teaches us what hospitality truly is. It's not about being perfect; it's about opening our hearts to each other and welcoming each other as we are.

PRAYER FOR THE THIRD SUNDAY OF ADVENT

Lord, listen to our prayers and by the grace of Your coming enlighten the darkness of our souls.

This we ask of You, Lord Jesus, living.

Amen

PRAYER FOR THE THIRD WEEK OF ADVENT

May God light the fire of His Love in our hearts.

Amen.

A HOME-MADE ADVENT WREATH CANDELABRA

This candelabra-style Advent Wreath is a more permanent version. It is a lot easier to make than you might think; it looks lovely too. One year, we made these Advent Wreaths for all the families on our Christmas list. Everyone was very impressed!

MATERIALS

- At least 32 inches of 1/2 inch copper plumbing pipe
- Four 90 degree copper elbows to fit the pipe
- Four copper T-joints to fit the pipe
- Four copper 1/2 inch to 3/4 inch joins (the narrow end should fit the pipe.)
- Pipe cutter
- Five-minute epoxy glue
- A large plate or platter
- Three purple candles
- One pink candle
- Four white candles (optional)
- Artificial garland, holly branches, branches from an artificial tree, pine cones, artificial berries, christmas tree ornaments, ribbons, other decorative items.

DIRECTIONS

1. Using the pipe cutter, cut the copper pipe into eight (8) three-inch sections and four (4) 1 1/2 inch sections (not shown below).

2. To cut pipe:

   a. Mark where you want to cut on the pipe.

   b. Place the copper pipe in the cutter, lining up your cut line with the little cutting wheel.

   c. Tighten the clamp onto the pipe.

   d. Rotate the pipe within the cutter, going around and around until the cutting wheel has cut a groove in the pipe.

   e. Tighten the clamp a bit and continue turning the pipe. The groove will deepen.

   f. Continue tightening and turning until the pipe is cut throught. Have patience, it will cut through!

3. Lay out all the pieces as shown below.

   a. The 3-inch pieces of pipe, elbows and top of the T joints form the base of the candelabra.

   b. The 1/2 to 3/4 joins and 1 1/2 inch pieces of pipe (not shown) are glued into the T joints and turned upright on the base to form the candle holders.

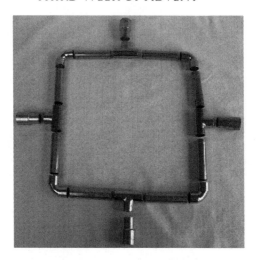

4. Following the directions on the glue package, prepare a small amount of epoxy glue (about a tablespoon).

5. Glue the copper pieces together, making sure the base is square and flat and that the candle holders are upright.

   a. Coat the inside of the join and the outside of the pipe with a small amount of epoxy. The fit is quite tight so if you use too much glue it will just squish out and get all over everything.

   b. Push the pieces together and twist them a few times to spread the glue evenly inside the joint. If you don't think there's enough glue, take it apart and add a little more.

   c. Mix and use more glue if necessary.

6. When the candelabra is assembled, put it aside to set. This may take a few hours or overnight; even though it's five-minute epoxy, these glue joins don't really have enough exposure to air to set in that time.

ALTERNATE ASSEMBLY METHOD

If you have a propane torch, flux and solder on hand, the candelabra can be soldered together.

It does take a deft touch to keep solder drips to a minimum, but it is fun to watch the solder get sucked into the joints!

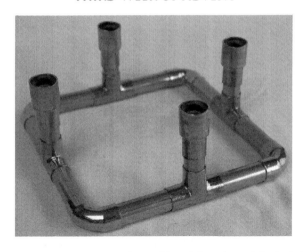

7. Your candelabra should look like this when it's finished.

8. Place the candelabra on a plate and add the candles. The plate makes it easier to move and catches any drips from the candles.

9. Arrange greenery so that some is trailing over the edges of the platter.

10. When you've finished adding the greenery, embellish your wreath with whatever you like. This wreath, though, also looks lovely with just a bit of greenery. The copper has a very nice glow to it especially by candlelight.

The Advent Wreath

THE FOURTH WEEK OF ADVENT: EVANGELIZATION

By the time we've reached the Fourth Sunday of Advent, we're almost ready!

All four candles are lit now. The Light of Christ is about to come into the world. Morning has broken. The people who walked in darkness will see a great light. And we can clearly see our dinner!

On the fourth week of Advent, it's time for the Light of Christ that's been growing brighter inside the home to start "shining out." It's time to start sharing this "Light of Christ" with the outside world.

Our house is easy to spot in the evenings during Advent.

Not only do we not have parties during Advent, we're the only house without lights.

Christmas lights are a celebratory thing. They're like fireworks in July, a big sign of celebration! So we reserve them for the Christmas season.

We put our lights up well before the snow flies (we DO live in Canada after all) but we don't turn them on until Christmas Eve. Then we light them every evening during the Christmas season, just as the time that everyone else is taking them down.

We're following St. Francis' advice to "preach the Gospel"; to evangelize without words.

Many of these activities demonstrate to our neighbours that our home and family is a domestic church and that we are honouring Advent as a special time set apart to prepare for the coming of the Christ Child. This raises curiousity and interest in the importance we place on our faith. We've "preached the Gospel" and evangelized without words.

PRAYER FOR THE FOURTH SUNDAY OF ADVENT

Rouse up Your power, Lord and come to us! Help us with all the strength of Your grace.

Then, by your bountiful mercy, we shall quickly be granted the blessings now denied us by our sins.

This we ask of You, Lord Jesus, living.

Amen

PRAYER FOR THE FOURTH WEEK OF ADVENT

May the King of Angels bring us to the company of the heavenly citizens.

Amen.

A HANGING ADVENT WREATH

This wreath is the most elaborate and complicated of all the Advent wreaths I'm suggesting in this book. It comes in handy though, if you've got a lot of people around the dinner table and space is at a premium.

MATERIALS

- Grapevine wreath (available from craft stores)
- Circle of cardboard or foamcore the same size as the grapevine wreath
- Roll of twine covered wire, brown florist's wire or other flexible wire
- Two-inch wide purple and rose ribbon
- Three purple candles
- One rose candle
- Four white candles (optional)
- Artificial garland, holly branches, branches from an artificial tree, pine cones, artificial berries, christmas tree ornaments, ribbons, other decorative items.

DIRECTIONS

1. Cut a hole out of the center of the cardboard or foamcore to make a "doughnut" shape the same size as the grapevine wreath.

2. Fasten the foamcore to the grapevine wreath with several lengths of wire (highlighted with black in the photo below). Wrap the wire around the foamcore and wreath and twist its ends together on the top of the wreath. They will be covered with greenery later.
   This strengthens and stabilizes the grapevine wreath.

3. Insert the candles into the wreath, pushing them through the grapevines down to the foamcore.
   Wiggle and push as necessary to get them firmly anchored and held in place by the vines.
   It can take quite a bit of wiggling and adjusting to get the candles securely held by the grapevines and at least approximately vertical (so that when lit, they don't drip too much...).

4. Next, create the hanging wires to the wreath by poking one end of a 24 to 30 inch long wire through the foam core and up through the center of the grapevine wreath. (highlighted with black in the photo.)

5. To keep the wire from pulling though, twist a knot on the bottom end of the wire. Depending on how you'll be hanging your wreath, make three or four hanging wires.

6. Begin to wrap greenery around the wreath, draping it from the sides of the wreath to cover and hide the foamcore layer.

7. When the wreath is covered with greenery, hang it! Secure the hanging wires to your candelabra, a hook in the ceiling, whatever you've chosen.

8. Next, cover the wires by wrapping them with the purple and rose ribbons. Make sure that the ribbons are not above the candles at any point; once lit you don't want to set the ribbons on fire!

The Advent Wreath

9. When you've finished arranging the ribbons, embellish your wreath with whatever you like.

THE CHRISTMAS SEASON: CELEBRATION

On Christmas Day, we replace the coloured candles on our Advent wreath with candles in the liturgical colors of white or gold.

White is a symbol of purity and gold is a symbol of celebration.

The wreath stays on our dinner table – with all four candles lit – through the Christmas season.

The charm and fascination of flickering candles brought into daily life speaks to the family quite clearly, saying Advent is a special time set apart to prepare for the coming of the Christ Child.

With the mission of the domestic church in mind, through the Advent wreath and other Advent observances that bring the Gospel message to life, we will become as families more fully what we are, become the cradle and setting of the Church, and truly live as incarnate beings, body and spirit.

Made in United States
Troutdale, OR
08/19/2025

33799277R00022